OUR SOCCER LEAGUE

Chuck Solomon

Crown Publishers, Inc., New York

For my mom and dad, Marie and Harold Solomon

The Falcons are: Mark Naison (Coach), Olivier Bagley, John Carpenito, Joely David, Danny Dimin, Kate Dimin, Matthew Hopkins, Eric Naison-Phillips, Jonathan Nuzum, Moira Poe, Toby Rappaport, and Samantha Winslow.

The Sluggers are: Rose Soussan (Coach), Christine Altman (Coach), Christopher Altman, Johnny Carroll, Richie Collins, Michael Gamanos, Brian Hart, Ted Hart, John Jasilli, Annie Levin, Noah Redlus, Ellie Soussan, David Trachtman, and Laura Trachtman.

Special thanks to Jeff Hecht, the Saint Saviour Youth Council, Mark Naison, Christine Altman, Tupper Thomas and the Prospect Park Administrator's Office—New York City Parks and Recreation, and to everyone else who makes Prospect Park, Brooklyn, the wonderful place it is for a game of soccer.

Copyright © 1988 by Chuck Solomon

Published by Crown Publishers, Inc., 225 Park Avenue South, New York 10003 and represented in Canada by the Canadian MANDA Group.

CROWN is a trademark of Crown Publishers, Inc.

Manufactured in Hong Kong.

Library of Congress Cataloging-in-Publication Data
Solomon, Chuck.
  Our soccer league.
  Summary: Text and photographs follow the Falcons and the Sluggers, two pony-cub soccer teams, as they prepare for and play the big game.
  1. Soccer—Juvenile literature.   [1. Soccer]
  I. Title.
GV943.25.S65   1988   796.334'2   88-10950

ISBN 0-517-56956-6

10 9 8 7 6 5 4 3 2 1

First Edition

We're the Falcons.

We play soccer!

Today the game is with our friends, the Sluggers. They wear blue shirts.

First everyone stretches.

Then we practice.
In soccer, you dribble the ball with your feet.

You pass to your teammates.

And you try to kick the ball through the goal, if you can.

Goalies need practice, too. They stop the other team from scoring, and they're the only players on the field who can touch the ball with their hands.

Falcons' goal

Out-of-bounds

Sluggers' goal

X Falcons (white shirts)
● Sluggers (blue shirts)

It's game time!
The coaches give us
our positions for the
opening kickoff.

The Sluggers kick off and burst downfield. They charge to the goal. There's a goal kick.

Defense! Our goalie,
Toby, makes a save.
Toby throws it out,
and we have the ball.

with the Sluggers in pursuit. Eric passes…

but a Slugger
intercepts!
He gets his foot
behind the ball…

and boots it!

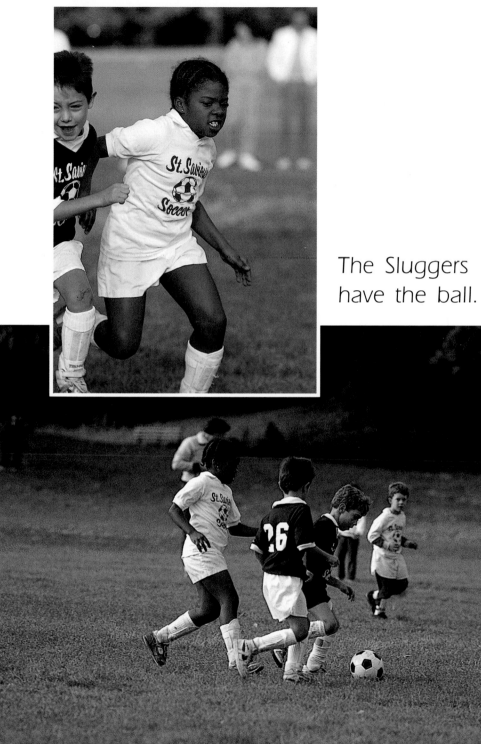

The Sluggers
have the ball.

But then it is kicked out-of-bounds.

Whenever a team puts the ball out,
the other team throws it back in.

Moira throws it
in for us.

"Don't use
your hands,
Johnny!"

Eric booms it.

Score! It's one to
nothing, Falcons.

Teams	1st half	2nd half	Final
FALCONS	1		
SLUGGERS			

But not for long.

The Sluggers
bounce right back
and tie the game.

It's now one to one.

Teams	1st half
FALCONS	1
SLUGGERS	1

The score is still tied at one to one when the coaches call half time.

Whew! It feels good to take a break.

After a ten-minute rest…

we're back to the game!

We charge down
to the Slugger's goal.

Olivier's kick is wide...

and the Sluggers
take the ball.

Here comes our
defense at midfield.
The two players collide.

It's anybody's ball.

The Sluggers
and Falcons battle
for the ball.

The ball
goes up...

Joely kicks it…

Oh, no! "Hand ball!"
Since a Slugger
touched the ball,
we get a free kick.

Jonathan booms it and
we have control again.

No one scored, and the clock is running out.
Only five minutes are left in the game.

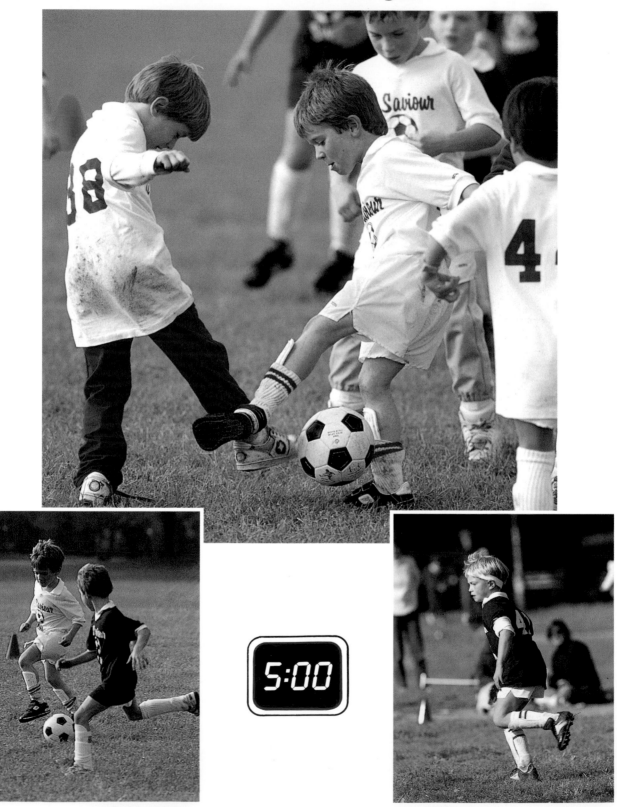

Out-of-bounds
on a header.

Ted throws it in.

The Sluggers boot the
ball into the open field.

2:00

John's set…boom!

Score! It's two to one, Sluggers!

We try our best
to tie the score ...

but the clock runs out.

Teams	1st half	2nd half	Final
FALCONS	1	0	1
SLUGGERS	1	1	2

The Sluggers celebrate…

and we give ourselves a cheer.

When you play a great game…

everybody wins!